STUDENT BOOK 2

T0383556

Linnette Ansel Erocak • Laura Miller

Series advisor: David Nunan

Pearson Education Limited
Edinburgh Gate
Harlow
Essex CM20 2JE
England
and Associated Companies throughout the world.

Poptropica English

© Pearson Education Limited 2015

Based on the work of Linnette Ansel Erocak

The rights of Laura Miller, and Linnette Erocak to be identified as authors of this work have been asserted by them in accordance with the Copyright, Designs and Patents Act 1988.

Stories on pages 16, 26, 38, 48, 60, 70, 82, and 92 by Catherine Prentice. The rights of Catherine Prentice to be identified as authors of this work have been asserted by them in accordance with the Copyright, Designs and Patents Act 1988.

Phonics syllabus and activities by Rachel Wilson

Editorial and project management by hyphen

First published 2015
Sixteenth impression 2020

ISBN: 978-1-292-09092-4

Set in Fiendstar 17/21pt

Printed in Slovakia by Neografia

Illustrators: Humberto Blanco (Sylvie Poggio Artists Agency), Anja Boretzki (Good Illustration), Scott Burroughs (Deborah Wolfe Ltd), Eva Byrne (The Bright Agency), Adam Clay, Lee Cosgrove, Leo Cultura, Joelle Dreidemy (The Bright Agency), Tom Heard (The Bright Agency), Marek Jagucki, Sue King (Plum Pudding Illustration), Daniel Limon (Beehive Illustration), Stephanine Lau, Yam Wai Lun, Katie McDee, Bill McGuire (Shannon Associates), Baz Rowell (Beehive Illustration), Mark Ruffle, Jackie Stafford, Olimpia Wong and Teddy Wong

Picture Credits: The Publishers would like to thank the following for their kind permission to reproduce their photographs: (Key: b-bottom; c-center, l-left; r-right; t-top)
123RF.com: 36/2, akulamatiau 41/1 (left), Jacek Chabraszewski 33 (girl), 40 (e), goodluz 28 (e), Sergey Kolesnikov 111/1, Dmytrii Minishev 93br, stockyimages 40 (h), Waroot Tangtumsatid 84/3, Gary Tognoni 110 (a); Alamy Images: DP RM 61/4, Jose Gil 111/3, Keith Morris 30tr, Photo Japan 111/2, Olga Volodina 30tc; Comstock Images: 94/4; Fotolia.com: babimu 93tc, Bernad 40 (i), brites_99 41/3 (left), Buriy 68/2, Jacek Chabraszewski 41/4 (right), Yanik Chauvin 62/5, Gennaro Coretti 36/5, Chepko Danil 94/3, Dar1930 93tl, demidoff 80/2, Mehmet Dilsiz 86/2, Joerg Dirmeitis 36/4, Daria Filiminova 28 (baby), fotofac 76l, Fotolyse 50bc, Gelpi 72/1, giideon 94/5, Scott Griessel 86/1, Mat Hayward 36/8, highwaystarz 107b, imagedb.com 41/4 (left), imagesetc 50bl, 71/1, indigolotos 80/10, iofoto 25r, Eric Isselée 58/2, katrinaelena 28 (a), Iculig 80/6, Liaurinko 80/7, Pavel Losevsky 40 (c), mayakova 30b, Monkey Business 107t, monticelllo 68/7, 71/2, Natika 61/3, 68/5, 74/3, 74/4, Olga Nayashkova 71/12, Sergey Novikov 93b (centre left), 94/2, Odua Images 91r, Tyler Olson 84/2, oriori 18b, Alexander Petrov 93tr, PictureArt 84/1, pixelrobot 68/10, Darya Prokapalo 110 (b), Elena Schweitzer 93b (centre right), somen 61/2, soupstock 36/6, spaxiax 68/6, 71/11, 74/5, Patrik Stedrak 62/3, Diana Taliun 68/9, underworld 62 (moon), verkoka 47 (Tom), vladakela 80/9, WavebreakmediaMicro 47 (Grandpa), Wisky 47 (Emma), www.1000tdw.com 110 (d), ztougas 62/1; Getty Images: Digital Vision / Rayes 30tl, iStock / Christopher Futcher 41t, KidStock 111/4, Photographer's Choice / Marcus Lyon 28 (twins), Stockbyte 28 (b); John Foxx Collection: Imagestate 62/6; MedioImages: 28 (d); Pearson Education Ltd: Studio 8 40 (d), 40 (f), 40 (l), 91l, Trevor Clifford 15l, 20, 21, 25l, 40 (a), 43tl, 49 (left), 50/1, 50/2, 50/3, 50/4, 50/5, 52, 59b, 76r, 87t, 87b, 104l, 104r, 105t, 105b, 106t, 106b, Miguel Domínguez Muñoz 47t, Tudor Photography 41/3 (right), 49 (right), 59t, Jules Selmes 40 (g), 40 (k), 41/2 (left), 41/2 (right), Rafal Trubisz 36/3, Ian Wedgewood 110 (c); Shutterstock.com: Ana Bokan 33 (a), Nina Buday 33 (c), Jacek Chabraszewski 40 (b), 41/1 (right), Coprid 80/5, Cre8tive Images 71/13, Alexander Dashewsky 68/4, 71/14, Sanjay Deva 86/4, Elenamiv 62 (sun), Elnur 80/8, 93bl, Jacek Fulawka 68/3, 74/2, Mandy Godbehear 36/7, Goodluz 28 (parents), 33 (d), gorillaimages 43 (swing), Hallgerd 40 (j), Pavel Hlystov 18c, Horiyan 61/1, iodrakon 47 (Aunt Jane), iofoto 84/4, Eric Isselee 58/3, 58/4, 58/5, Ivan Kuzmin 62/4, Maceofoto 71/6, MarcusVDT 36/1, MariusdeGraf 71/10, Rob Marmion 72/2, mexrix 71/9, Monkey Business Images 28 (c), 28 (g), Juriah Mosin 43 (swim), MShev 43tr, Maks Narodenko 71/5, Sergey Peterman 71/4, pio3 94/1, Valentina Razumova 71/3, Mikhail Rulkov 50br, shooarts 80/1, Shout It Out Design 62/2, Somchai Som 71/8, Alex Staroseltsev 68/1, StockLite 33 (b), Marek R. Swadzba 80/4, Magdalena Szachowska 43 (climb), Max Topchii 28 (f), Suzanne Tucker 43 (dance), Richard Upshur 28 (h), Kirsanov Valeriy Vladimirovich 58/1, Valentyn Volkov 68/8, 71/7, 74/1, Chamille White 80/3, Tracy Whiteside 15r, 86/3, Mark Yuill 18t; Stockdisc: 28 (grandparents); www.imagesource.com: Nigel RIches 72/3

All other images © Pearson Education

Every effort has been made to trace the copyright holders and we apologize in advance for any unintentional omissions. We would be pleased to insert the appropriate acknowledgement in any subsequent edition of this publication.

Contents

Scope and sequence

Welcome

Vocabulary:	**Time:** one o'clock, two o'clock, three o'clock, four o'clock, five o'clock, six o'clock, seven o'clock, eight o'clock, nine o'clock, ten o'clock, eleven o'clock, twelve o'clock **Daily routines:** wake up, get up, eat breakfast, go to school, eat lunch, eat dinner, go to bed
Structures:	What time is it? It's one o'clock. I wake up at six o'clock.

1 My toys

Vocabulary:	**Toys:** teddy bear, car, kite, doll, boat, bike, ball, truck, train **Numbers:** 16–50	**Values:** Friendship is important. **Cross-curricular:** **Math:** plus, minus, and equals
Structures:	What's this/that? It's a bike. It's yellow. What are these/those? They're bikes. They're yellow. How many bikes are there? There are sixteen bikes.	**Phonics: ch, sh** chop, ship

2 My family

Vocabulary:	**Family members:** grandson, uncle, aunt, granddaughter, son, daughter, cousin **Neighborhood places:** house, yard, bakery, post office, restaurant, apartment	**Values:** Spend time with your relatives. **Cross-curricular:** **Social science:** Types of family members
Structures:	Who's he/she? He's/She's my uncle/aunt. Where's my/your uncle? Your/My uncle is in the house.	**Phonics: th, th** this, thin

3 Move your body

Vocabulary:	**Actions:** point, wave, move, nod, shake, sit down, turn around, touch **Physical abilities:** jump, swim, dance, climb, swing, stand on your head, do cartwheels, do the splits	**Values:** Exercise regularly. **Cross-curricular:** **Health:** Exercise actions
Structures:	Touch your toes. Can you jump? Yes, I can. / No, I can't Can he/she jump? Yes, he/she can. / No, he/she can't.	**Phonics: ng, nk** sing, pink

4 My face

Vocabulary:	**Parts of the body:** face, hair, eyes, ears, mouth, nose **Hairstyles:** long, short, curly, straight, wavy, dark, blond, red, neat, messy	**Values:** Respect differences. **Cross-curricular:** **Math:** Shapes
Structures:	I have a small nose. He/She has a small nose. Do you have a small nose? Yes, I do. / No, I don't. Does he/she have a small nose? Yes, he/she does. / No, he/she doesn't. He/She has long hair. His/Her hair is long.	**Phonics: ai, ee** tail, sheep

5 Animals

Vocabulary:	**Farm animals:** horse, sheep, cow, turkey, chicken, goat, goose, pig, duck **Wild animals:** bat, crow, skunk, owl, fox
Structures:	What's this/that? It has big eyes. It's black and white. It's a cow. Is it small? Yes, it is. / No, it isn't. Is it a bat? Yes, it is. / No, it isn't. Are the bats big? Yes, they are. / No, they aren't.

Values: Respect animals.

Cross-curricular:
Science: Daytime and nighttime animals

Phonics: igh, oa
high, goat

6 Food

Vocabulary:	**Food items:** rice, hot dogs, eggs, chicken, burgers, pizza, bananas, apples, pineapple, coconut, pumpkin, corn, toast, cereal, grapes, beans, raisins, nuts
Structures:	What's your favorite food? My favorite food is pizza. I like chicken. I don't like eggs. He/She likes pineapple for breakfast. He/She doesn't like pineapple for breakfast. Does he/she like pineapple for breakfast? Yes, he/she does. / No, he/she doesn't.

Values: Eat good food. Choose good snacks.

Cross-curricular:
Social science: Different cultures, different foods

Phonics: oo, oo
zoo, book

7 Clothes

Vocabulary:	**Clothes:** dress, skirt, shoes, socks, pants, T-shirt, shirt, coat, sweater, hat, cap, boots, pajamas, jeans, sneakers, shorts
Structures:	I'm wearing a white skirt. I'm not wearing white pants. What do you want? I want a shirt, please. Do you want a blue shirt? Yes, I do. / No, I don't. I want a red shirt.

Values: Be polite.

Cross-curricular:
Social science: Occupations and uniforms

Phonics: ar, ir, or, ur
car, girl, corn, fur

8 Weather

Vocabulary:	**Weather:** sunny, cloudy, snowy, rainy, windy, cool **Days of the week:** Sunday, Monday, Tuesday, Wednesday, Thursday, Friday, Saturday **Activities:** ride a bike, fly a kite, make a snowman, go for a walk, go to the beach, read a book, take a picture, watch TV
Structures:	Do you like cloudy days? Yes, I do. / No, I don't. I like cloudy days. I don't like cloudy days. What day is it today? It's Sunday. What's the weather like? It's sunny.

Values: Share with friends and family.

Cross-curricular:
Science: Temperature

Phonics: ow, oy
owl, boy

Welcome

1 **A:02** Listen and write.

2 **A:03** Listen and circle.

AWESOME HELPER AWARD

1 Charlie

2 Rose

3 Ola

4 Uncle Dan

3 **Look and match.**

1 yellow
2 red

3 green
4 blue

5 orange
6 pink

a
b
c
d
e
f

4 **Listen and chant.** A:04 / A:05

Hello, Rose. How are you?
I'm fine, thank you.
And how are you?
Hello, Charlie. How are you?
I'm fine, thank you.
And how are you?

5 **Listen and number.** A:06

a
b
c
d
e
f
g
h

6 **A:07** **Listen and say.**

| one o'clock | two o'clock | three o'clock | four o'clock | five o'clock | six o'clock |

| seven o'clock | eight o'clock | nine o'clock | ten o'clock | eleven o'clock | twelve o'clock |

7 **A:08 / A:09** **Listen and chant. Then draw.**

CHANT

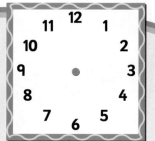

(1) What time is it? What time is it?
It's time to get up. Get out of bed!
What time is it? What time is it?
It's seven o'clock. It's seven o'clock.

(2) What time is it? What time is it?
It's time to go to school, my friend!
What time is it? What time is it?
It's eight o'clock. It's eight o'clock.

(3) What time is it? What time is it?
It's time to eat lunch. I want some bread!
What time is it? What time is it?
It's one o'clock. It's one o'clock.

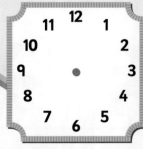

(4) What time is it? What time is it?
It's time to go to bed, sleepy head!
What time is it? What time is it?
It's ten o'clock. It's ten o'clock.

8 Listen and circle.
Then ask and answer.

LOOK!

What time is it?

It's one o'clock.

1

2

3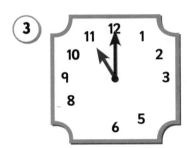

4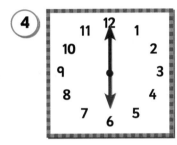

What time is it?

It's four o'clock.

9  **Look and write.**

1

It's _____ o'clock.

2

It's _____ o'clock.

3

It's _____ o'clock.

10 **Look, listen, and number.**

a
wake up

b
get up

c
eat breakfast

d
go to school

e
eat lunch

f
eat dinner

g
go to bed

11 **Listen and match. Then write.**

1 wake up	twelve o'clock	I _____ at twelve o'clock.
2 get up	seven o'clock	I _____ at seven o'clock.
3 eat breakfast	five o'clock	I _____ at five o'clock.
4 go to school	eight o'clock	I _____ at eight o'clock.
5 eat lunch	six o'clock	I **wake up** _____ at six o'clock.
6 eat dinner	nine o'clock	I _____ at nine o'clock.
7 go to bed	ten o'clock	I _____ at ten o'clock.

Look and write about yourself.

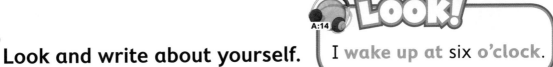
LOOK!
A:14
I **wake up at** six **o'clock**.

1 I wake up at _____ o'clock.

2 I get up at _____.

3 I eat _____ at _____.

4 I go to _____
at _____.

5 I _____ at _____.

  Look. Listen and sing.
A:15

  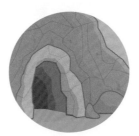 

Quest
A:15

1 My toys

1 ⭐ **What do you know?**

TOYS

teddy bear

car

boat

bike

doll

truck

train

2 🎧 A:16 **Listen and find.**

3 🎧 A:17 **Listen and circle.**

4 🎧 A:18 **Listen and say.**

Can identify toys

5  **Listen and chant.**

What's this? It's red.
It's a car.

What's that? It's blue.
It's a boat.

What are these? They're brown.
They're teddy bears.

What are those? They're purple.
They're kites.

kite

HELP
AT THE
CASTLE

ball

LOOK!

A:21

What's this/that?	It's a bike. It's yellow.
What are these/those?	They're bikes. They're yellow.

6 **Listen and number. Then ask and answer.**

a

these

b

that

c

this

d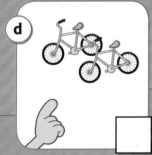

those

What's this?

It's a ball.
It's orange.

(7)  **Listen and say.**

16 sixteen   **17** seventeen   **18** eighteen   **19** nineteen

20 twenty   **30** thirty   **40** forty   **50** fifty

(8)  **Listen and write the number. Then sing.**

SONG

Trains, trains,
How many trains?
How many trains are there?
Seventeen trains.
Seventeen trains.
I can see seventeen trains.

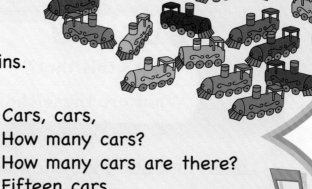

Cars, cars,
How many cars?
How many cars are there?
Fifteen cars.
Fifteen cars.
I can see fifteen cars.

Balls, balls,
How many balls?
How many balls are there?
Twenty balls.
Twenty balls.
I can see twenty balls.

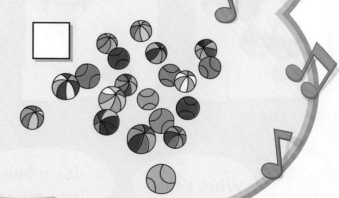

9 **Look and circle.**
Then ask and answer.

How many bikes **are there?**

There are sixteen bikes.

1

(nineteen / fifteen)

2

(seventeen / sixteen)

3

(twelve / twenty)

4

(fourteen / eighteen)

How many trains
are there?

There are
nineteen trains.

WRITING

10  **Look at Activity 9. Write.**

1 How many trains are there?

There are _____ trains.

2 How many teddy bears are there?

There are _____ teddy bears.

3 How many dolls are there?

There are _____ dolls.

4 How many trucks are there?

There are _____ trucks.

Listen to the story. Read.

12 **Role-play the story.**

Can understand a simple story / Can role-play a story

13 **Listen. Then number in order.**

VALUES

 Friendship is important.

14 **Look and check (✓). Then write about yourself.**

Good friends play together and share toys.

Good friends listen and help.

Who is your best friend? What do you like?

_____ is my best friend.

We like _____,

but we don't like _____.

15  Look and write.

1	2	3	4	5	6	7	8		10
11		13		15		17	18		20

16 Listen and stick. Then say.

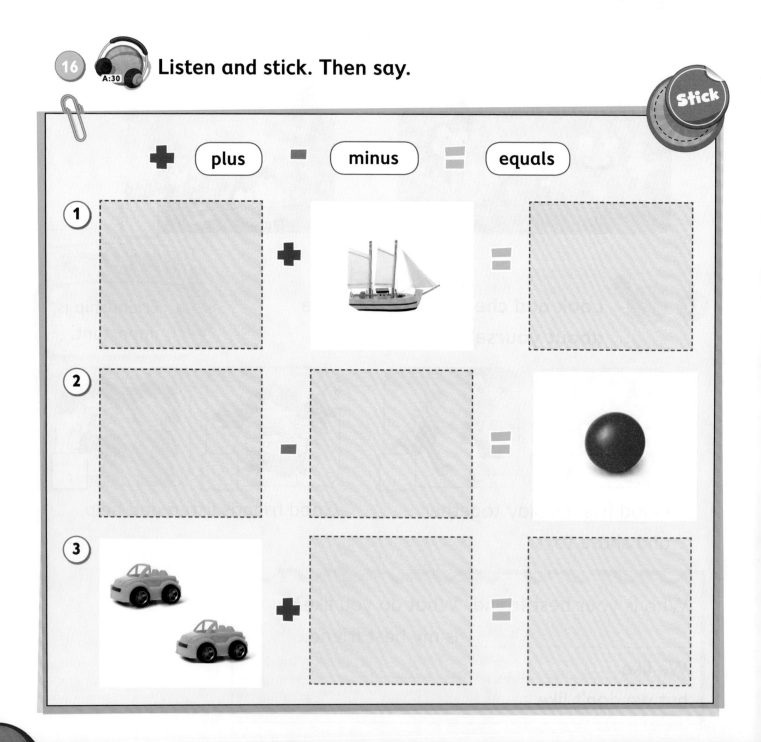

17 Draw or find pictures of toys.
Write + (plus), - (minus), and = (equals).

18 Make a math problems poster for a friend.
Give the poster a title.

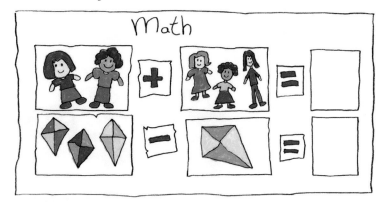

HOME SCHOOL LINK

Share your math problems with your family.

19  Listen.

① **chop** ② **ship**

20  Listen and blend the sounds.

21  Circle *ch* and *sh*. Read the words aloud.

1 shell **2** chop **3** rich **4** fish **5** chin **6** ship

22 **Listen and write the numbers.**

 **a** **16**

 **b**

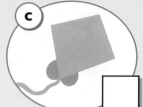 **c**

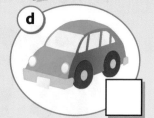 **d**

 **e**

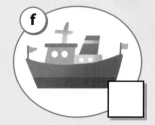 **f**

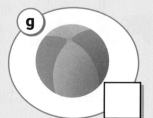 **g**

 **h**

  23 **Read and circle. Then say.**

1 (What's this? / What are these?)
(It's a truck. / They're trucks.)

2 How many (kites / cars) are there?
There are (fifteen / twenty).

  24 **Look at Activity 22. Choose. Then ask and answer.**

How many teddy bears are there?

There are sixteen teddy bears.

25 **Listen. Then play.**

What are these?

They're kites.

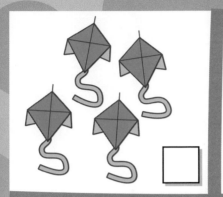

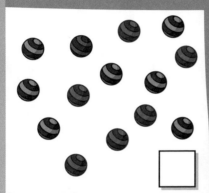

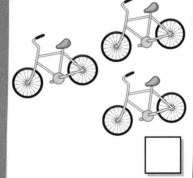

26 **Look at Activity 25. Count and write. Then ask and answer.**

How many cars are there?

There are two cars.

Now go to Poptropica English World

2 My family

1 **What do you know?**

HELP WITH DINNER

grandson

2  **Listen and find.**

3  **Listen and circle.**

4 **Listen and say.**

Can identify family members

5  Listen and chant.
A:38 / A:39

Who's he? He's my grandpa.
Who's she? She's my aunt.
Who's he? He's my uncle.
Who's she? She's Ola!
Who are they? They're my cousins.
They're my family. Hey, hey!

uncle

aunt

son

daughter

granddaughter

cousin

A:40 **LOOK!**

Who's he/she? He's/She's my uncle/aunt.

Who's = Who is

6 A:41 Listen and number. Then repeat.

a

b

c

Quest
A:42

7 **Stick. Then listen and say.**

1
house

2
yard

3
bakery

4
post office

5
restaurant

6
apartment

8 **Listen and match. Then sing.**

Where's my grandma? Where's my grandma?
She's in the house. Snore, snore, snore.
Where's my grandma? Where's my grandma?
She's in the house. Snore, snore, snore.

Where's my cousin? Where's my cousin?
He's in the yard. Play, play, play.
Where's my cousin? Where's my cousin?
He's in the yard. Play, play, play.

Where's my daughter? Where's my daughter?
She's in the bakery. Buy, buy, buy.
Where's my daughter? Where's my daughter?
She's in the bakery. Buy, buy, buy.

Where's my uncle? Where's my uncle?
He's in the restaurant. Eat, eat, eat.
Where's my uncle? Where's my uncle?
He's in the restaurant. Eat, eat, eat.

a

b

c

d

Can identify places in the neighborhood

9 **Listen and match.**
Then ask and answer.

LOOK!

Where's my uncle?	Your uncle is in the house.
Where's your uncle?	My uncle is in the house.

1 Where's my mom?

2 Where's my grandma?

3 Where's my uncle?

4 Where's my aunt?

5 Where's my grandson?

6 Where's my cousin?

a

b BAKERY

c 23

d POST OFFICE

e YARD

f RESTAURANT

Where's my mom?

Your mom is in the house.

SPEAKING

10  **Complete for yourself. Then ask a friend.**

aunt   cousin   grandma   uncle

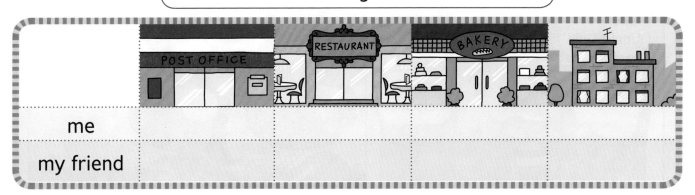

	POST OFFICE	RESTAURANT	BAKERY	
me				
my friend				

Where's your grandma?

My grandma is in the post office.

Can ask and answer about where somebody is

Listen to the story. Read.

12 **Role-play the story.**

Can understand a simple story / Can role-play a story

13  **Read and write.**

MY FAMILY

Charlie

14  **Read and write. Then draw your relatives.**

How many aunts do you have?

_____

How many uncles do you have?

_____

How many cousins do you have?

_____

15   **Listen and point. Then say.**

SOCIAL SCIENCE

young

baby

twins

parents

old

grandparents

16  **Look and match.**

a

b

c

d

1 twins

2 parents

3 babies

4 grandparents

e

f

g

h

Can identify more family members

17 Draw pictures of your family.
Label the pictures.

18 Make a poster about your family. Give the poster a title.

Display your poster at home.

19  Listen.

① **this**　② **thin**

20  Listen and blend the sounds.

21  Circle *th*. Read the words aloud.

1 math　　**2** this　　**3** that　　**4** path　　**5** thick　　**6** thin

22 **Listen and check (✓). Ask a friend.**

A:52

I CAN DO IT!

1 a ✓ b ☐

2 a ☐ b ☐

3 a ☐ b ☐

4 a ☐ b ☐

5 a ☐ b ☐

6 a ☐ b ☐

23 **Draw a relative.**
Then write and say.

Where's your _____?
My _____ is in the _____.

24 **Choose. Then ask and answer.**

Where's your sister?

My sister's in the bakery.

25 **Ask and answer.**

26 **Look at Activity 25. Then write.**

1 Where's your mom? My mom is in the _____.

2 Where's your dad? My dad is in the _____.

3 Where's your grandma? My grandma is in the _____.

4 Where's your grandpa? My grandpa is in the _____.

Now go to Poptropica
English World

Lesson 10 Can use what I have learned in Unit 2   31

Review  Units 1 and 2

1  **Listen and draw. Then write.**

1  I wake up at _____ o'clock.

2  I go to school at _____ o'clock.

3 I eat dinner at _____ o'clock.

2 **Read and circle. Then write.**

1

What's (this / that)?
It's a _____.

2

What are (these / those)?
They're _____.

3

What are (these / those)?
They're _____.

4

What's (this / that)?
It's a _____.

3 **Write.**

 16    19    20    40

1 s____n   **2** n__t__   **3** t____y   **4** f____

Can talk about my toys

4 **A:54** **Listen and number.**

a

b

c

d

5 **A:55** **Write. Then listen and match.**

1

2

3

4

BAKERY

POST OFFICE

a _____

b _____

c _____

d _____

3 Move your body

1 ⭐ What do you know?

move

wave

point

sit down

shake

5 A:59 / A:60 **Listen and chant.**

Arms, arms, wave your arms,
Wave your arms with me.

Toes, toes, touch your toes,
Touch your toes with me.

Nod, nod, nod your head,
Nod your head with me.

Legs, legs, move your legs,
Move your legs with me.

Turn around.
Move, wave, shake.
And sit down!

HELP
AT THE
CAVE

nod

touch

turn around

A:61 **LOOK!**
Touch your toes.

6 A:62 **Listen and number. Then say.**

a

b

c

d

Quest A:63

7 **Listen and do. Then say.**

VOCABULARY

jump

swim

dance

climb

swing

stand on your head

do cartwheels

do the splits

8 **Listen and ✓ or ✗. Then sing.**

SONG

Can you jump?
Yes, I can.
Can you jump?
Yes, I can.
Can you jump?
Yes, I can.
I can jump! Hooray!

Can you climb?
No, I can't.
Can you climb?
No, I can't.
Can you climb?
No, I can't.
I can't climb. Boo hoo!

Can you swim?
Yes, I can.
Can you swim?
Yes, I can.
Can you swim?
Yes, I can.
I can swim! Hooray!

Can you dance?
No, I can't.
Can you dance?
No, I can't.
Can you dance?
No, I can't.
I can't dance. Boo hoo!

I can...

jump. ☐   climb. ☐   swim. ☐   dance. ☐

Can identify actions

LOOK!

A:67

| Can you jump? | Yes, **I can**. / No, **I can't**. |
| Can he/she jump? | Yes, **he/she can**. / No, **he/she can't**. |

3

9 Look, read, and circle. Then ask and answer.

1 Can you do cartwheels?

(Yes, I can. /
No, I can't.)

2 Can you do the splits?

(Yes, I can. /
No, I can't.)

3 Can you swim?

(Yes, I can. /
No, I can't.)

Can he do cartwheels?

Yes, he can.

10 Complete for yourself. Then ask a friend.

WRITING

	do cartwheels	do the splits	stand on your head	swing	swim
me					
my friend					

11 Write about yourself and a friend.

I can _____. I can't _____.

My friend can _____.

He/She can't _____.

Lesson 4

Can ask and answer about things you can do

37

13 **Role-play the story.**

14 **Read and number. Then match.**

a

Jump! Touch your toes!

☐

b

Swing! Do the splits! Move your body!

☐

or

c

Move your feet! Stand on your head!

☐

d

Stand on one leg! Turn around!

☐

VALUES

👍 Exercise regularly.

15 **Look and stick.**

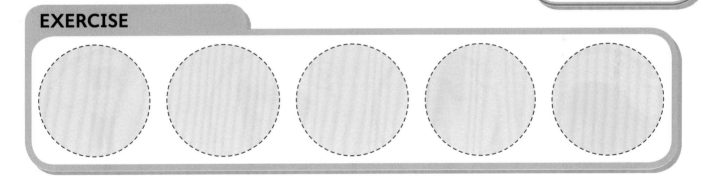

EXERCISE

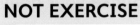 

NOT EXERCISE

Stick

16 **Listen and number. Then say.**

a

b

c

d

pull · push · hop · jump rope

 17 **Listen and number. Then move.**

a

b

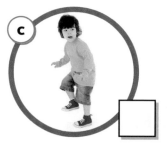
c

d

Clap your hands. · Jump. · Stamp your feet. · Wave your arms.

e

f

g

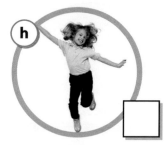
h

Move your head. · Dance. · Touch your toes. · Shake your body.

i

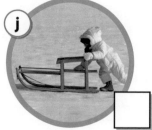
j

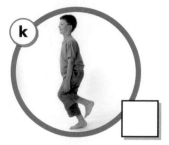
k

l

Pull. · Push. · Hop. · Jump rope.

Can identify more body movements

18 Work in small groups. Choose some actions to make an exercise routine.

19  Listen. Then show the class an exercise routine.

①

②

③

④

HOME SCHOOL LINK
Share your exercise routine with your family.

20 Listen.

① **sing** ② **pink**

 PHONICS

21  Listen and blend the sounds.

22  Circle *ng* and *nk*. Read the words aloud.

  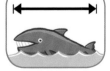   

1 pink   **2** sing   **3** long   **4** sink   **5** ring   **6** ink

23 A:74 **Listen and number. Ask a friend.**

a ☐ b ☐ c ☐ d ☐ e ☐ f ☐

24 🖌 **What can you do? Draw. Then write and say.**

I can _____.

I can't _____.

25 A:75 **Listen and check (✓).**

1
a ☐ b ☐

2
a ☐ b ☐

3
a ☐ b ☐

4
a ☐ b ☐

26 **Choose and say. Then do.**

wave

touch

point

move

shake

Touch your toes!

27 **Ask a friend and check (✓). Then say.**

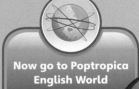

Now go to Poptropica
English World

4 My face

1 ⭐ **What do you know?**

hair

face

eyes

mouth

nose

ears

2 🎧 **Listen and find.**

3 🎧 **Listen and circle.**

4 🎧 **Listen and say.**

Can identify parts of the face

5 B:05/B:06 Listen and chant.

HELP THE DOCTOR

Do you have small eyes?
No, I don't.

Do you have big eyes?
Yes, I do!

Does he have short hair?
No, he doesn't.

Does he have long hair?
Yes, he does!

Does she have a big nose?
No, she doesn't.

Does she have a small nose?
Yes, she does!

ARRIVALS

B:07 **LOOK!**

I have a small nose.	**He/She has** a small nose.
Do you have a small nose?	Yes, **I do.** / No, **I don't.**
Does he/she have a small nose?	Yes, **he/she does.** / No, **he/she doesn't.**

6 B:08 Listen and draw. Then draw yourself and say.

girl

me

I have big eyes.

Quest B:09

Can ask and answer about parts of the face using *have*

7 B:10 **Stick. Then listen and say.**

 1 long

 2 short

 3 curly

 4 straight

 5 wavy

 6 dark

 7 blond

 8 red

 9 neat

 10 messy

Stick

8 B:11 / B:12 **Listen and number. Then sing.**

SONG

1 Who is it? Who can it be?
Who is it? Listen to me!
She has blue eyes, blue eyes,
And a small nose, a small nose.
She has small ears, small ears,
And long, straight hair.
Who is it? It's Susie!

2 Who is it? Who can it be?
Who is it? Listen to me!
He has brown eyes, brown eyes,
And a small nose, a small nose,
He has a big mouth, a big mouth,
And short, curly hair.
Who is it? It's Tommy.

3 Who is it? Who can it be?
Who is it? Listen to me!
She has green eyes, green eyes,
And a big nose, a big nose.
She has big ears, big ears,
And neat, blond hair.
Who is it? It's Mary!

a  ☐

b  ☐

c  ☐

Can identify ways to describe hair

 **9** Listen and number. Then say.

a  □

b □

c  □

d  □

He has blond hair.
His hair is messy.

10  Look, write, and circle.

 **WRITING**

Grandpa   Emma   Tom   Aunt Jane

1 Who is it?

It's _____. (His / Her) hair is straight and blond.

2 Who is it?

It's _____. (His / Her) hair is dark and curly.

3 Who is it?

It's _____. (His / Her) hair is short and curly.

4 Who is it?

It's _____. (His / Her) hair is short and straight.

Listen to the story. Read.

1
Let's find the new doctor. His name is Tim.

Is he nice?

2
Does he have long hair?

No, his hair is short.

3
Does he have messy hair?

No, he doesn't!

This is for you.

4
Does he have blue eyes?

I don't know, but he has glasses.

Do you have blue eyes?

5
Er, can he swim?

Oops! Sorry!

6
Hello, I'm the new doctor.

Oh! Welcome to Tropical Island!

Role-play the story.

Can understand a simple story / Can role-play a story

13 **Read and circle. Then check (✓).**

1 Does Tim have long hair? (Yes, he does. / No, he doesn't.)

2 Does Tim have short hair? (Yes, he does. / No, he doesn't.)

3 Does Tim have messy hair? (Yes, he does. / No, he doesn't.)

4 Does Tim have glasses? (Yes, he does. / No, he doesn't.)

14 **Complete for yourself. Then ask a friend.**

VALUES

me

my friend

Respect differences.

15 **Write about yourself.**

Yes, I do.

I have _____.
Do you have curly hair?

1
circle

2
triangle

3
square

4
rectangle

5
It's a face!

17 **Count and write.**

_____ circles

_____ triangle

_____ squares

_____ rectangles

_____ triangles

_____ squares

_____ rectangles

_____ circle

18 Draw shapes in different sizes.
Color the shapes different colors.

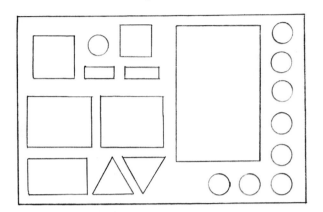
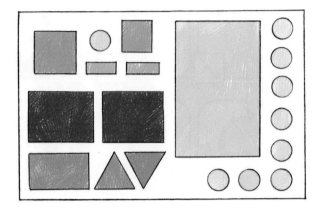

19 Cut out the shapes. Make a picture with shapes.

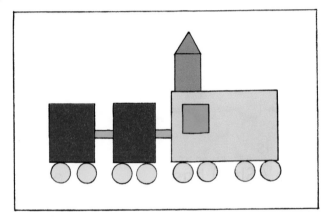

Make another picture with shapes at home.

20  Listen.

1 **tail** 2 **sheep**

21  Listen and blend the sounds.

22 Circle *ai* and *ee*. Read the words aloud.

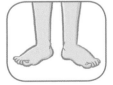

1 feet **2** rain **3** mail **4** sheep **5** tail **6** week

23  Listen and check (✓).

B:19

1 a b
2 a b
3 a b

4 a b
5 a b
6 a b

24 Draw a friend. Then write.

This is _____.
(He / She) has _____ eyes,
_____ hair, a _____
nose, and a _____ mouth.

25 Choose from Activity 23. Then ask and answer.

She has short, gray hair.
Her eyes are small.

It's 4 a!

I CAN DO IT!

Can assess what I have learned in Unit 4

26 **Draw. Then circle and write.**

My drawing

(He / She) has _____ eyes.

(He / She) has a _____ mouth.

(He / She) has _____ ears.

(He / She) has a _____ nose.

(He / She) has _____ hair. (long/short)

(He / She) has _____ hair. (color)

(He / She) has _____ hair. (wavy/curly/straight)

27 **Ask, answer, and check (✓). Then draw.**

Does she have big eyes?

Yes, she does.

My friend's drawing

eyes	☐ big	☐ small	
mouth	☐ big	☐ small	
ears	☐ big	☐ small	
nose	☐ big	☐ small	
hair	☐ long	☐ short	
	☐ straight	☐ curly	☐ wavy
	☐ dark	☐ blond	☐ red

Now go to Poptropica English World

Review Units 3 and 4

1 B:20 Listen and check (✓).

1

a ☐   b ☐

2

a ☐   b ☐

3

a ☐   b ☐

4

a ☐   b ☐

5

a ☐   b ☐

6

a ☐   b ☐

2 Write.

1

She can _____ _____.

2

He _____ _____.

3

He _____ _____.

4

She _____ _____.

5

He _____ _____.

6

She _____ _____.

Can talk about body movements and actions

3  **Listen and draw.**

1
boy

2
girl

4 **Listen and write.**

Simon

Ann

Bob

Sally

1   Who is it? It's _____.

2   Who is it? It's _____.

3   Who is it? It's _____.

4   Who is it? It's _____.

5   Who is it? It's _____.

5 Animals

 1 What do you know?

sheep

horse

turkey

goose

pig

duck

2  B:23 Listen and find.

3 B:24 Listen and circle.

4  B:25 Listen and say.

Can identify farm animals

5 🎧 B:26 / B:27 **Listen and chant.**

What's this? What's this?
It has a big nose.
It's big and gray.
It's a horse! Yes!

What are these? What are these?
They have two legs.
They're small and brown.
They're chickens! Yes!

cow

goat

HELP THE FARMER

chicken

🎧 B:28 **LOOK!**

What's this/that?

It has big eyes.
It's black and white.
It's a cow.

6 🎧 B:29 **Listen and number. Then ask and answer.**

a

b

c

d

What's this?
It has long legs.
It's black and white.

It's a cow.

Quest B:30

7 B:31 Stick. Then listen and say.

1

bat

2

crow

3

skunk

4

owl

5

fox

TIP!
one fox
two foxes

 Stick

8 B:32 / B:33 Listen and match. Then sing.

SONG

Chorus:
I'm Max. And I'm Maisie.
We're animal crazy!

1 What's this?
What's this?
It's small and green.
It has big eyes.
It's a frog!

(Chorus)

2 What are these?
What are these?
They're black and white.
They have a tail.
They're skunks!

(Chorus)

3 What's that?
What's that?
It's small and gray.
It has two wings.
It's a bat!

(Chorus)

4 What are those?
What are those?
They're thin and black.
They have two legs.
They're crows!

(Chorus)

a

b

c

d

Can identify wild animals

 **LOOK!**

| Is it small? Is it a bat? | Yes, it is. / No, it isn't. |
| Are the bats big? | Yes, they are. / No, they aren't. |

5

9  **Listen and circle. Then ask and answer.**

Is it a fox?

(Yes, it is. /
Yes, they are.)

Yes, it is.

(No, it isn't. /
No, they aren't.)

(No, it isn't. /
Yes, it is.)

(Yes, they are. /
No, they aren't.)

SPEAKING

10 **Choose. Then ask and answer.**

Is it small?

Yes, it is.

12   **Role-play the story.**

Can understand a simple story / Can role-play a story

13 **Read and circle.**

1

Are cows big?

(Yes, they are. / No, they aren't.)

2

Is that a sheep?

(Yes, it is. / No, it isn't. It's a goat.)

3

Are these turkeys?

(Yes, they are. / No, they aren't. They're chickens.)

4

Are horses VERY big?

(Yes, they are. / No, they aren't.)

VALUES

Respect animals.

14 **Show how animals help us.**
Look and stick.

1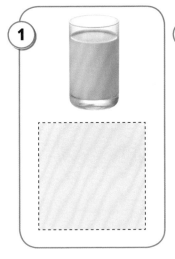

2

3

4

Stick

15 **Listen and point. Then say.**

B:37

SCIENCE

1

2

3

4

5

6

16  **Read and find. Then write.**

1 It's brown.
It's awake at night.

It's a _____.

2 It has two legs and a big head.
It's asleep in the day.

It's an _____.

3 It's black and white.
It's awake in the day.

It's a _____.

4 It has two legs.
It's asleep at night.

It's a _____.

Can talk about when animals are awake and asleep

PROJECT

17 Draw or find pictures of different animals. Label the pictures.

18 Make a poster about animals. Give your poster a title.

HOME SCHOOL LINK

Share your poster with your family.

PHONICS

19 Listen. **B:38**

1 high **2** goat

20 Listen and blend the sounds. **B:39**

21 Circle *igh* and *oa*. Read the words aloud.

1 boat   **2** high   **3** goat   **4** light   **5** soap   **6** coat

22   **Listen and number. Ask a friend.**

a

b

c

d

23 **Draw an animal. Then ask and answer.**

Is it big?

Is it thin?

24  **Read and match. Then write.**

1 It's fat. It has four legs.

a  **b**

2 It's big. It's gray.
It has four legs.

3 It has short legs.
It has wings.

c  **d**

4 It's big. It's black and white.
It's fat.

Can assess what I have learned in Unit 5

25 **Circle the one that doesn't belong. Say.**

1

2

3

4

5

Now go to Poptropica
English World

Lesson 10

Can use what I have learned in Unit 5

65

1 ⭐ What do you know?

HELP WITH THE SHOPPING

rice — $1.50

hot dogs — $1.75

chicken — $6.00

burgers — $2.50

pizza — $2.50

eggs — $3.00

bananas

apples

2 Listen and find.

3  Listen and circle.

4 Listen and say.

Can identify food items

5 Listen and chant.

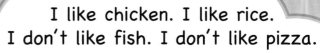

> I like chicken. I like rice.
> I don't like fish. I don't like pizza.
>
> I like eggs. I like apples.
> I don't like bananas. I don't like burgers.
>
> What's your favorite food?
> My favorite food is hot dogs!

LOOK!
B:46

What's your favorite food?	My favorite food is pizza.
I like chicken.	I don't like eggs.

6 Look and write. Then draw and say.

1

I like _____ .

2

I don't like _____ .

3

I don't like _____ .

4

I like _____ .

My favorite food

I like _____

_____ .

B:47

7 Listen and say.

 **1** pineapple

 **2** coconut

 **3** pumpkin

 **4** corn

 **5** toast

 **6** cereal

 **7** grapes

 **8** beans

 **9** raisins

 **10** nuts

 8 Listen and circle. Then sing.

SONG

I eat breakfast, I eat lunch, I eat dinner. How about you?
I eat breakfast, I eat lunch, I eat dinner. How about you?

I like / and / , too.

I like / . How about you?

I like / . My favorite dish!

But I don't like / !

(Chorus)

I like / and / , too.

I like / . How about you?

I like / . It's very nice.

But I don't like  / !

(Chorus)

Can identify more food items

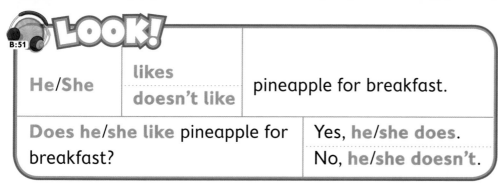

He/She	likes	pineapple for breakfast.
	doesn't like	
Does he/she like pineapple for breakfast?	Yes, he/she does.
	No, he/she doesn't.

9 **Look and circle. Then ask and answer.**

1 She (likes / doesn't like) toast for breakfast.

2 Does he like grapes for breakfast? (Yes, he does. / No, he doesn't.)

3 Does he like corn for lunch? (Yes, he does. / No, he doesn't.)

Does she like toast for breakfast?

Yes, she does.

10  **B:52** **Listen and stick. Then say.**

SPEAKING

1

2

She likes cereal for breakfast.

I like toast and grapes for breakfast.

Stick

11   B:53 **Listen to the story. Read.**

1

I like pineapple for breakfast.

Mmm. I like apples.

I like bananas.

2

I like apple juice.

I like milk.

I like banana milkshakes.

drinks

3

I like burgers for dinner. What do you like, Uncle Dan?

Ha! I like chicken and rice.

4

My favorite cake is chocolate cake.

Yum! My favorite is apple cake.

Well, I like banana cake.

BAKERY

5

Pizza for me, please.

A salad for me, please. What does Ola like?

6

BANANAS!!

12   **Role-play the story.**

Can understand a simple story / Can role-play a story

13  **Read and check (✓).**

		YES	NO
1	Charlie likes apple juice.	☐	☐
2	Rose doesn't like apples.	☐	☐
3	Uncle Dan likes pineapple for lunch.	☐	☐
4	Ola likes banana milkshakes.	☐	☐
5	Charlie's favorite cake is chocolate cake.	☐	☐
6	Uncle Dan likes chicken and rice for dinner.	☐	☐
7	Rose likes milk.	☐	☐
8	Charlie likes salad for dinner.	☐	☐

14 **Look and circle the good food and snacks.**

VALUES

Eat good food. Choose good snacks.

1 2 3 4

5 6 7 8 9

10 11 12 13 14

15 **Read, look, and match. Then say.**

1   2

3

a   I like eggs, tortillas, and juice for breakfast.

b   I like noodles, vegetables, and tea for breakfast.

c   I like croissants, yogurt, and coffee for breakfast.

16 **Complete for yourself. Then ask a friend and write.**

What's your favorite food?

I like chicken and salad for dinner.

	NAME	DINNER
1	Me	
2	Friend	chicken and salad
3		
4		
5		

17 **Show and tell a friend.**

My friend likes chicken and salad for dinner.

18 Draw or find pictures of your favorite lunch or dinner. Label the pictures.

19 Make a poster of your favorite lunch or dinner. Give your poster a title.

HOME SCHOOL LINK

Help to make your favorite meal at home.

20  **B:54** Listen.

PHONICS

① **zoo** ② **book**

21 **B:55** Listen and blend the sounds.

22 Underline *oo*. Read the words aloud.

1 moon **2** cook **3** zoo **4** foot **5** book **6** food

23 Look and write. Ask a friend.

1. _____
2. _____
3. _____

What's your favorite food?

Do you like pumpkin?

4. _____
5. _____

24 B:56 Listen and check (✓).

1. a ☐   b ☐
2. a ☐   b ☐
3. a ☐   b ☐
4. a ☐   b ☐

25 Ask a friend and circle. Then draw.

Do you like beans for lunch?

No, I don't.

burgers	grapes
chicken	nuts
hot dogs	apples
pizza	pumpkin
beans	corn

Can assess what I have learned in Unit 6

26 Play the game.

 =

 =

 =    =

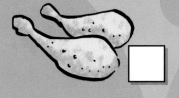 ☐

 ☐

 ☐

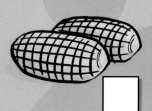 ☐

 ☐

 ☐

27  **Write. Then ask and answer.**

1 I like _____ and _____ for breakfast.

2 I like _____ and _____ for dinner.

> Do you like apples for breakfast?

> Yes, I do.

28  **Write.**

1 My friend likes _____ and _____ for breakfast.

2 My friend likes _____ and _____ for dinner.

Now go to Poptropica
English World

 1 **Ask and answer.**

It's thin. It's gray. It has four legs.

It's a goat!

 2 **Write.**

①

②

③

It's a _____.   It's an _____.   It's a _____.

It's _____.   It's _____.   It's _____.

It has _____.   It has _____.   It has _____.

Can talk about animals

3 **Listen and number. Then say for you.**

a  ☐

b  ☐

c  ☐

d  ☐

> I like eggs and toast, but I don't like yogurt.

> I like eggs, toast, and bananas.

 **4** **Listen and circle.**

1

2

Can talk about food likes and dislikes   77

7 Clothes

1 ⭐ **What do you know?**

HELP WITH THE CLOTHES

dress

skirt

shoes

2 🎧 B:59 **Listen and find.**

3 🎧 B:60 **Listen and circle.**

4 🎧 B:61 **Listen and say.**

Can identify clothes

5 Listen and chant.

I'm wearing a purple skirt,
A purple skirt, a purple skirt.
I'm wearing a purple skirt.
How about you?

I'm not wearing green shoes,
Green shoes, green shoes.
I'm not wearing green shoes.
They're brown, brown, brown.

I'm not wearing pink socks,
Pink socks, pink socks.
I'm wearing white socks.
How about you?

T-shirt

pants

ocks

LOOK!

I'm wearing a white skirt.
I'm not wearing white pants.

6 Listen and color. Then say.

1

2

3

I'm wearing a yellow
dress and red shoes.

Can describe what I'm wearing

7 **Listen and say.**
B:67

1
shirt

2
coat

3
sweater

4
hat

5
cap

6
boots

7
pajamas

8
jeans

9
sneakers

10
shorts

8 **Listen and number. Then sing.**
B:68/
B:69

 SONG

1 Good morning!
Good morning!
Take off your pajamas.
It's time for school.

2 Put on your shirt.
Put on your jeans.
Put on your sneakers.
Off you go!
It's time for school.

3 Good night!
Good night!
Put on your pajamas.
It's time for bed.

4 Take off your hat.
Take off your sweater.
Take off your boots.
Off you go! It's time for bed.
Good night! Good night!
Good night! Good night!

a □   b □   c □   d □

LOOK!

What do you want?	I want a shirt, please.
Do you want a blue shirt?	Yes, I do. / No, I don't. I want a red shirt.

9 Listen and circle. Then ask and answer.

1

2

3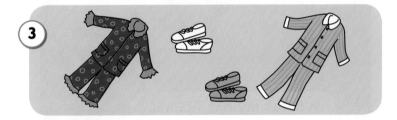

What do you want?

I want boots, please.

Do you want brown boots?

No, I don't. I want red boots, please.

10 Listen and stick. Then ask and answer.

LISTENING

I want...

I don't want...

Stick

Do you want a black T-shirt?

No, I don't. I want a white T-shirt.

1 Where's my hat? Do you have my hat? — It isn't here.

2 I'm wearing pants. Where's my dress? — Oh, my. — And where's my HAT?!

3 Do you want this pink dress? — No! My dress is blue!

4 Nice dress! — Oh! Thank you! — Where's my hat, PLEASE?

5 These are for you. — Ooh! Nice hats!

6 Thank you. You are very kind. Here, take this umbrella. — Thank you!

  Role-play the story.

Can understand a simple story / Can role-play a story

13 **Read, look, and match.**

1 I'm wearing pants. Where's my dress?

2 Do you want this pink dress?

3 Where's my hat? Do you have my hat?

4 These are for you.

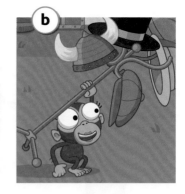

VALUES

Be polite.

14 **Look and stick.**

Stick

SOCIAL SCIENCE

I'm a firefighter. I'm wearing a helmet.

I'm a chef. I'm wearing a white hat.

I'm a nurse. I'm wearing a white dress.

I'm a police officer. I'm wearing a badge.

1

firefighter

2

chef

3

nurse

4

police officer

16  **Listen and number.**

a

b

c

d

17 Draw a picture of someone wearing a uniform. Label the clothes.

18 Make a poster describing a uniform. Give your poster a title.

19  Listen.

PHONICS

① car **②** girl **③** corn **④** fur

20  Listen and blend the sounds.

21 Underline *ar, ir, or,* and *ur*. Read the words aloud.

1 shark   **2** corn   **3** girl   **4** surf   **5** car   **6** fur

22 Listen and match.

 1

 **2**

 **3**

 4

 **a**

 **b**

 **c**

 **d**

 23 Draw and color your clothes. Then write.

I'm wearing _____

_____

_____ .

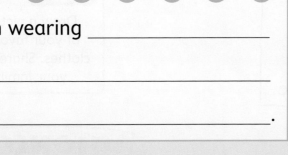 **24** Listen and check (✓).

 **1** **a**

 **b**

 **2** **a**

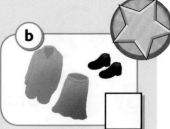 **b**

 **3** **a**

 **b**

 **4** **a**

 **b**

Can assess what I have learned in Unit 7

25 **Color and say.**

I want
red socks.

26 **Look and write.**

I want _____

_____

_____.

Now go to Poptropica
English World

Lesson 10

Can use what I have learned in Unit 7

87

8 Weather

snowy

 1 What do you know?

sunny

cloudy

windy

HELP AT THE MOUNTAIN

 **2** Listen and find.

 **3** Listen and circle.

 **4** Listen and say.

Can identify types of weather

5 C:05 / C:06 🎧 **Listen and chant.**

rainy

SUNDAY	
MONDAY	
TUESDAY	
WEDNESDAY	
THURSDAY	
FRIDAY	
SATURDAY	

Do you like sunny days?
Sunny days, sunny days?
Do you like sunny days?
Yes, I do!

Do you like rainy days?
Rainy days, rainy days?
Do you like rainy days?
No, I don't!

Do you like snowy days?
Snowy days, snowy days?
Do you like snowy days?
Yes, I do!

C:07 🎧 **LOOK!**

| Do you like cloudy days? | Yes, **I do.** / No, **I don't**. |
| **I like** cloudy days. | **I don't like** cloudy days. |

cool

6 C:08 🎧 **Listen and draw. Then say.**

1 2 3 4

Quest C:09

7 **Listen and say.**

1
ride a bike

2
fly a kite

3
make a snowman

4
go for a walk

5
go to the beach

6
read a book

7
take a picture

8
watch TV

8 **Listen and number. Then sing.**

1 What day is it today?
It's Monday. Monday!
What's the weather like?
It's sunny. It's sunny.
Let's go for a walk!

2 What day is it today?
It's Friday. Friday!
What's the weather like?
It's snowy. It's snowy.
Let's make a snowman!

3 What day is it today?
It's Wednesday. Wednesday!
What's the weather like?
It's windy. It's windy.
Let's fly a kite.

I like sunny days,
I like windy days.
I like snowy days,
Let's have fun and play.

a

b

c

| What day is it today? | It's Sunday. |
| What's the weather like? | It's sunny. |

9 Listen, circle, and draw. Then ask and answer.

1 Sunday Monday Tuesday
Wednesday Thursday
Friday Saturday

It's windy.
It's cool.
It's sunny.

2 Sunday Monday Tuesday
Wednesday Thursday
Friday Saturday

It's cloudy.
It's sunny.
It's windy.

3 Sunday Monday Tuesday
Wednesday Thursday
Friday Saturday

It's snowy.
It's rainy.
It's cool.

What day is it today?

It's Tuesday.

What's the weather like?

It's sunny.

10  Write about yourself.

What day is it today? _____

What's the weather like? _____

Do you like _____ days? (Yes / No), I _____ .

  Role-play the story.

13 Number the pictures in order. Then write.

a

It's _____.

b

It's _____.

c

It's _____.

d

It's _____.

14 Circle what you can share.

VALUES

👍 Share with friends and family.

15   **Listen and point. Then write and say.**

1 freezing

2 cold

3 warm

4 hot

°C
50
40
30
20
10
0
-10
-20

_____

_____

_____

_____

16  **Listen. Then write.**

1
It's sunny.
It's _____.
Let's _____.

2

3
It's windy.
It's _____.
Let's _____.

It's cloudy.
It's _____.
Let's _____.

4
It's snowy.
It's _____.
Let's _____.

5
It's rainy.
It's _____.
Let's _____.

17 Draw pictures of weather conditions. Color the pictures.

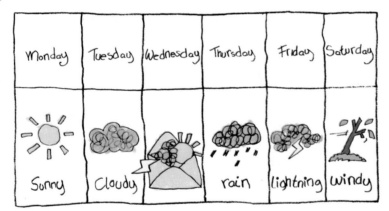

18 Make a weather chart. Write the days of the week.

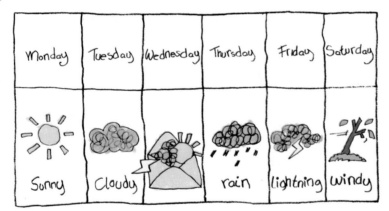

Monday	Tuesday	Wednesday	Thursday	Friday	Saturday
Sunny	Cloudy		rain	lightning	windy

HOME SCHOOL LINK

Take your weather chart home and complete for every day of the week.

19  **C:18** Listen.

PHONICS

1  owl   **2**  boy

20  **C:19** Listen and blend the sounds.

21  Underline *ow* and *oy*. Read the words aloud.

1 boy   **2** owl   **3** toy   **4** cow   **5** cowboy   **6** down

22 **Write. Then listen and number.**

It's _____ .   It's _____ .   It's _____ .   It's _____ .   It's _____ .

Monday	Tuesday	Wednesday	Thursday	Friday

23 **Draw yourself on your favorite day. Then write.**

It's _____ .

It's _____ .

I like _____ days.

Let's _____ .

24 **Listen and check (✓).**

1   **a**    **b**    2   **a**    **b**

3   **a**    **b**    4   **a**    **b**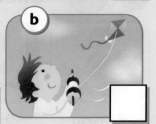

25 **Listen. Then play.**

26 **Listen and act.**

Review Units 7 and 8

1 ✏️ **Read and write the number.**

a **b** **c** **d**

1   I'm wearing a sweater and jeans.

2   I'm wearing pants and a hat.

3   I'm wearing a skirt and socks.

4   I'm wearing a T-shirt and pants.

2 🎧 C:24 **Listen and number.**

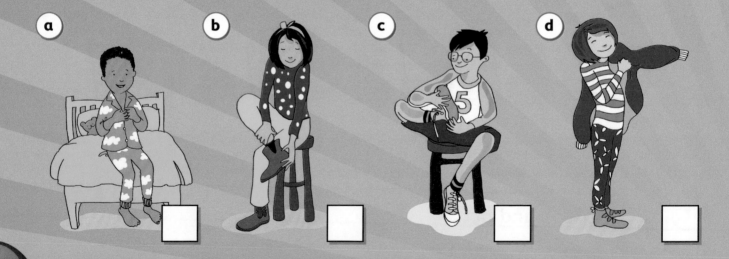

a **b** **c** **d**

Can talk about clothes

3  Write.

1 S _ _ _ _ _	**2** M _ _ _ _ _
3 _ _ _ d _ _	**4** W _ _ _ _ _ _ _ _
5 _ _ _ s _ _ _	**6** F _ _ _ _ _
7 _ a _ _ _ _ _ _	

4 Listen and draw. Then write.

C:25

1

It's _____ .

Let's _____ .

2

It's _____ .

Let's _____ .

3

It's _____ .

Let's _____ .

4

It's _____ .

Let's _____ .

Goodbye

1 **Listen, find, and circle.**

2 **Listen and number.**

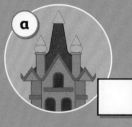
a

b

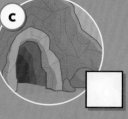
c

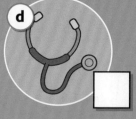
d

e

f

g

h

Can identify food

③  Who is at the party? Write.

1 _____   2 _____   3 _____

4 _____   5 _____   6 _____

7 _____   8 _____   9 _____

4 **Listen and number. Then write.**
C:28

in   on   under

a

She _____ the cave.

b

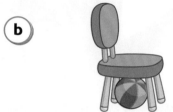

It's _____ the chair.

c

They're _____ the table.

d

He's _____ the castle.

 **5** **Read, look, and circle. Then ask and answer.**

1

Where (is / are) the socks?

2

Where (is / are) the doll?

3

Where (is / are) the teddy bear?

4

Where (is / are) the cars?

Where's the teddy bear?

It's in the box.

Can ask and answer about where things are

6  **Listen and sing.**

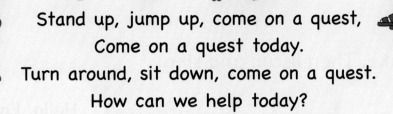

Stand up, jump up, come on a quest,
Come on a quest today.
Turn around, sit down, come on a quest.
How can we help today?

At the castle, with dinner, at the cave, the doctor, the farmer,
With the shopping, with the clothes, at the mountain
We can help today!

Rose and Charlie are home again,
And Ola's happy today – Hooray!
Rose and Charlie are home again,
And Ola's happy today – Hooray!
Hooray! Hooray! Hooray!
Hooray! Hooray! Hooray!

7  **Draw five of your favorite things. Then show and tell.**

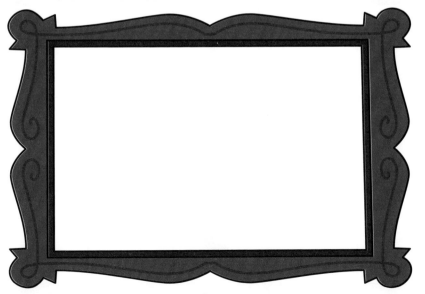

Goodbye!

Easter

1 **Make. Then listen and sing.**

Hello, Easter Bunny.
How are you today?
Wake up, wake up,
Come and play.

Jump, jump, jump,
Easter Bunny jump!
Turn around, turn around,
Fall down with a thump.

(x2)

2 **Play the game.**

rabbit

egg

 chick

flower

1			2		
1			**1**		
2			**2**		
3			**3**		

Can make an Easter Bunny and sing an Easter song

Christmas

1 **Listen and sing. Then find and say.**

star

stocking

Christmas tree

present

Santa

Hang up your stockings
By the Christmas tree.
Hang up your stockings,
It's Christmas Eve.
It's Christmas Eve.

Who's this with a brown sack
In the living room?
With a long white beard
And a big red nose,
And he laughs with a ho, ho, ho!

Is it true? Can it be?
Yes, It's Santa! Come and see.
With a long white beard
And a big red nose
And presents for you and me.

(Chorus)

2 **Make and play.**

Happy holidays!

Valentine's Day

  Listen and sing. Then find and say.

balloon   heart   flower   chocolates

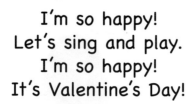

I'm so happy!
Let's sing and play.
I'm so happy!
It's Valentine's Day!

Here's a flower for my mom.
Some chocolates for my dad.
Here's a heart for Grandma,
And a card for Grandpa.

(Chorus)

2 **Make and say.**

Two hearts!

Halloween

1 **Listen and sing. Then find and say.**

candy

jack-o'-lantern

witch

Come on! It's Halloween!
It's time to trick-or-treat!
The moon is smiling up there,
And the stars are out there.
Do you have some yummy candy
Ready for me?
Are you a ghost or a scary witch?
Jack-o'-lanterns smile at me!

(x2)

2 **Prepare. Then have a party.**

Wider World 1

Cousins

My name's Amy. I have six cousins. They're all different.

1 Read and match.

1 This is my uncle and aunt with my cousin Harry. Harry is a baby. They live in Australia!

2 These are my cousins Ella and Jack. Ella is a girl, and Jack is a boy. They are with their parents in this picture. They live in a house.

3 These are my cousins Daisy and Louise. They're twins! They live in an apartment, but in this picture they are in the yard.

4 And this is my cousin Matt. He's eight years old. He lives here in America. He has a treehouse!

a

b

c

d

2  Ask and answer.

How many cousins do you have?

Where do they live?

What are their names?

How old are they?

3  Write about a cousin. How old is he/she? Where does he/she live?

Can understand descriptions of families around the world

Wider World 2

World sports

1 **Read and write.**

a

soccer player

b

gymnast

c

basketball player

d

ballet dancer

e

athlete

1 She can do the splits, and she can point her toes.

2 He can kick a ball, and he can run fast.

3 He can swing and touch his toes.

4 She can run fast, and she can jump.

5 He can catch and throw a ball. He can jump.

d

2  **Play a guessing game.**

Can you jump?

Yes, I can.

Can you kick a ball?

Are you an athlete?

No, I can't.

3  **Write about a sports person from another country.**

Wider World 3

Life on a farm

1 **Read and match.**

1
My name's Grace. I live in South Africa. I live on an ostrich farm!

2
Ostriches are big birds. They have big bodies and long legs. They can run fast, but they can't fly. The father is black. What color is the mother?

3
These are ostrich eggs. They're very big. How many eggs can you see?

4
These are ostrich chicks. They're funny. What color are they?

a **b** **c** **d**

2  **What farm animals are there in your country? Look and circle.**

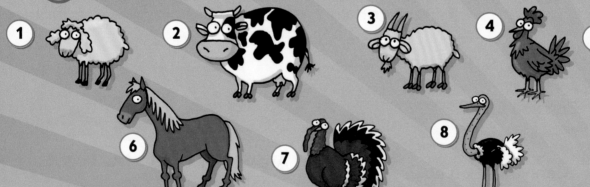

1   2   3   4   5   6   7   8

3  **Write about a farm animal in your country. Make a class booklet.**

Wider World 4

Special clothes

1 Read and check (✓).

When do you wear special clothes?

At a birthday party?

At a festival?

For New Year's?

For Halloween?

2 Look, read, and write the numbers.

a My name's Chun. This is me with my friends. I'm wearing black trousers and a white T-shirt. We have a dragon puppet!

b My name's Olivia. It's my birthday! I'm wearing a pretty pink dress.

c My name's Brandon, and this is my friend Michael. I'm wearing a white shirt and a black hat. We have pumpkins!

d I'm Takumi. This is me and my sister. Her name's Ami. I'm wearing a long brown skirt and a coat. Ami is wearing a blue dress with white shoes.   **2**

3  Ask and answer.

When do you wear special clothes?

What do you wear?

4  Design some special clothes. Make a class booklet.

Picture dictionary

Numbers

 sixteen

 seventeen

 eighteen

 nineteen

 twenty

 thirty

 forty

 fifty

Days of the week

Sunday **Monday** **Tuesday** **Wednesday** **Thursday** **Friday** **Saturday**

Time

 one o'clock

 two o'clock

 three o'clock

 four o'clock

 five o'clock

 six o'clock

 seven o'clock

 eight o'clock

 nine o'clock

 ten o'clock

 eleven o'clock

 twelve o'clock

a

apartment
p. 24

apples
p. 66

aunt
p. 22

b

bakery
p. 24

ball
p. 12

bananas
p. 66

bat
p. 58

beans
p. 68

bike
p. 12

blond
p. 46

boat
p. 12

boots
p. 80

burgers
p. 66

c

cap
p. 80

car
p. 12

cereal
p. 68

chicken
p. 56

chicken
p. 66

climb
p. 36

cloudy
p. 88

coat
p. 80

coconut
p. 68

cool
p. 88

corn
p. 68

Picture dictionary

cousin ....
p. 22

cow ....
p. 56

crow ....
p. 58

curly ....
p. 46

d

dance ....
p. 36

dark ....
p. 46

daughter ....
p. 22

do cartwheels ....
p. 36

do the splits ....
p. 36

doll ....
p. 12

dress ....
p. 78

duck ....
p. 56

e

ears ....
p. 44

eat breakfast ....
p. 10

eat dinner ....
p. 10

eat lunch ....
p. 10

eggs ....
p. 66

eyes ....
p. 44

f

face ....
p. 44

fish ....
p. 68

fly a kite ....
p. 90

fox ....
p. 58

g

get up ....
p. 10

goat
p. 56

go for a walk
p. 90

go to bed
p. 10

go to school
p. 10

go to the beach
p. 90

goose
p. 56

granddaughter
p. 22

grandson
p. 22

grapes
p. 68

h

hair
p. 44

hat
p. 80

horse
p. 56

hot dogs
p. 66

house
p. 24

i

j

jeans
p. 80

jump
p. 36

k

kite
p. 12

l

long
p. 46

m

make a snowman
p. 90

messy
p. 46

mouth
p. 44

move
p. 34

n

neat
p. 46

nod
p. 34

nose
p. 44

nuts
p. 68

o

owl
p. 58

p

pajamas
p. 80

pants
p. 78

pig
p. 56

pineapple
p. 68

pizza
p. 66

point
p. 34

post office
p. 24

pumpkin
p. 68

q

r

rainy
p. 88

raisins
p. 68

read a book
p. 90

restaurant
p. 24

rice
p. 66

ride a bike
p. 90

s

shake
p. 34

sheep
p. 56

shirt

p. 80

shoes

p. 78

short

p. 46

shorts

p. 80

sit down

p. 34

skirt

p. 78

skunk

p. 58

sneakers

p. 80

snowy

p. 88

socks

p. 78

son

p. 22

stamp

p. 40

stand on your head

p. 36

store

p. 26

straight

p. 46

sunny

p. 88

sweater

p. 80

swim

p. 36

swing

p. 36

take a picture

p. 90

teddy bear

p. 12

toast

p. 68

touch

p. 34

train

p. 12

truck

p. 12

T-shirt ....
p. 78

turkey ....
p. 56

turn around ....
p. 34

u

uncle ....
p. 22

v

w

wake up ....
p. 10

watch TV ....
p. 90

wave ....
p. 34

wavy ....
p. 46

windy ....
p. 88

x

y

yard ....
p. 24

z

Acknowledgments

The Publishers would like to thank the following teachers for their suggestions and comments on this course:

Nurhan Deniz, Alejandra Juarez, Lara Ozer, Cynthia Xu, Basia Zarzycka

Jennifer Dobson, Anabel Higuera Gonzalez, Honorata Klosak, Dr Marianne Nikolov, Regina Ramalho

Asako Abe, JiEun Ahn, Nubia Isabel Albarracín, José Antonio Aranda Fuentes, Juritza Ardila, María del Carmen Ávila Tapia, Ernestina Baena, Marisela Bautista, Carmen Bautista, Norma Verónica Blanco, Suzette Bradford, Rose Brisbane, María Ernestina Bueno Rodríguez, María del Rosario Camargo Gómez, Maira Cantillo, Betsabé Cárdenas, María Cristina Castañeda, Carol Chen, Carrie Chen, Alice Chio, Tina Cho, Vicky Chung, Marcela Correa, Rosalinda Ponce de Leon, Betty Deng, Rhiannon Doherty, Esther Domínguez, Elizabeth Domínguez, Ren Dongmei, Gerardo Fernández, Catherine Gillis, Lois Gu, SoRa Han, Michelle He, María del Carmen Hernández, Suh Heui, Ryan Hillstead, JoJo Hong, Cindy Huang, Mie Inoue, Chiami Inoue, SoYun Jeong, Verónica Jiménez, Qi Jing, Sunshui Jing, Maiko Kainuma, YoungJin Kang, Chisato Kariya, Yoko Kato, Eriko Kawada, Sanae Kawamoto, Sarah Ker, Sheely Ker, Hyomin Kim, Lee Knight, Akiyo Kumazawa, JinJu Lee, Eunchae Lee, Jin-Yi Lee, Sharlene Liao, Yu Ya Link, Marcela Marluchi, Hilda Martínez Rosal, Alejandro Mateos Chávez, Cristina Medina Gómez, Bertha Elsi Méndez, Luz del Carmen Mercado, Ana Morales, Ana Estela Morales, Zita Morales Cruz, Shinano Murata, Junko Nishikawa, Sawako Ogawa, Ikuko Okada, Hiroko Okuno, Tomomi Owaki, Sayil Palacio Trejo, Rosa Lilia Paniagua, MiSook Park, SeonJeong Park, JoonYong Park, María Eugenia Pastrana, Silvia Santana Paulino, Dulce María Pineda, Rosalinda Ponce de León, Liliana Porras, María Elena Portugal, Yazmín Reyes, Diana Rivas Aguilar, Rosa Rivera Espinoza, Nayelli Guadalupe Rivera Martínez, Araceli Rivero Martínez, David Robin, Angélica Rodríguez, Leticia Santacruz Rodríguez, Silvia Santana Paulino, Kate Sato, Cassie Savoie, Mark Savoie, Yuki Scott, Yoshiko Shimoto, Jeehye Shin, MiYoung Song, Lisa Styles, Laura Sutton, Mayumi Tabuchi, Takako Takagi, Miriam Talonia, Yoshiko Tanaka, María Isabel Tenorio, Chioko Terui, José Francisco Trenado, Yasuko Tsujimoto, Elmer Usaguen, Hiroko Usami, Michael Valentine, José Javier Vargas, Nubia Margot Vargas, Guadalupe Vázquez, Norma Velázquez Gutiérrez, Ruth Marina Venegas, María Martha Villegas Rodríguez, Heidi Wang, Tomiko Watanabe, Jamie Wells, Susan Wu, Junko Yamaguchi, Dai Yang, Judy Yao, Yo Yo, Sally Yu, Mary Zhou, Rose Zhuang

Unit 1 My toys
page 18

Unit 2 My family
page 24

Unit 3 Move your body
page 39

Unit 4 My face

page 46

Unit 5 Animals

page 58

page 61

Unit 6 Food

page 69